Rutgers University—PUBLICATIONS OF THE ONE HUNDRED SEVENTY-FIFTH ANNIVERSARY CELEBRATION
Number One

The Bases of Artistic Creation

THE BASES OF
Artistic Creation

Essays by

MAXWELL ANDERSON
RHYS CARPENTER · ROY HARRIS

New Brunswick
RUTGERS UNIVERSITY PRESS
1942

Printed in the United States of America

Contents

The Bases of Artistic Creation

The Basis of Artistic Creation in Literature

MAXWELL ANDERSON

SOME apology is necessary for the presentation of a paper in academic circles which is written without awareness of the winds of thought at present swirling through academic halls. Perhaps the word swirling is too strong to describe what is happening to philosophic thinking in the colleges and universities, but I doubt it. Nowadays all the bases of thinking are attacked by the champions of might makes truth, and all those who are capable of considering their position in the world are making a re-examination of the dilemma of mankind, an ancient dilemma, but one which looks different in different lights, and looks appallingly grim in the light of civilization on fire and burning down. Each of us faces this catastrophe from his own point of view – and with his own limitations of vision. The professor of philosophy is less open to influences of the market place, more likely to have considered all aspects of the problem, than the professional writer or artist. On the other hand, he doesn't feel the same driving necessity for finding an immediate and workable theory of what's going on. A student can comment on the riddles of destiny without arriving at any conclusion, but a practicing artist or a professional writer who uses ideas in his work is bound to conclude something, make-shift or profound, or shut up shop completely.

And a playwright, who must say something intelligible in every production, is driven more directly than any other writer or artist to make up his mind about his world or be silent until he can make up his mind. A man would be a fool who was certain that his vision of current events was the only right one, who believed that he had come upon the secret of the universe, or who thought he had penetrated, for certain, to the basis of artistic creation in literature or anywhere else. But if he is going to put plays on the stage he must have at least fragmentary convictions concerning all three of those things. Sometimes his convictions are subconscious; sometimes they are inherited. Sometimes the convictions that underlie the most modern and snappy of productions are simple-minded or old-fashioned. But dig for them, and you will find them. A play can't be written without them – or, at least, it can't be a success – because no audience is satisfied with a play which doesn't take an attitude toward the world. Every artist is at a loss in a confused civilization, but the playwright is in the worst plight of all. For the best practice of his craft he needs a stable society within a stable congeries of nations. Our modern world has been the scene of vast mental and social confusion, and the theatre has been shaken to its foundations with every shift in the ideological weather. Those who have kept going as writers within it have done so because they could cling to inner beliefs not easily destroyed by exterior storm. Or because they believed in nothing and could simulate whatever belief happened to be popular. This paper is an attempt to indicate what has so far given me nerve to write words to be spoken on the American stage. I can't be sure whether or not such an attempt has accurate bearing on today's discussion. What other writers use to keep them going I can only guess by inference or analogy. But if I am to speak at all on this subject I must make the unwarranted assumption that the experiences of most playwrights have been similar to mine, and that literature as a whole is created somewhat as plays are written.

Those who are old enough to remember the nineteen-twenties will recall one curious fallacy of that decade, a belief more extraordinary than the prosperity that accompanied it. The victory over Germany and the efflorescence of invention that went with and followed the war staggered men's minds. They saw the earth and its creatures in a bright new scientific light in which the customs of our ancestors appeared to be based on inexplicable and ridiculous taboos. Religion was not only questioned, but put aside. Social codes were scrutinized under microscopes, and scrapped along with the rules of Leviticus. There was a general belief that men were done with the foolishness of wars and conquest as a method of settling differences. On this side of the Atlantic at least, we thought men had learned better than to try again to grasp the steering wheel of the earth by violence. We closed our eyes to smoking volcanoes of malignity, wondering foolishly how men would adjust themselves to a life in which there was no more hell fire. We believed that the war had been a mistake, that no war was worth fighting, even for the victor; that Gandhi was right, that non-resistance was more powerful than force, that the conqueror destroyed himself automatically, that good and evil came in unavoidable waves, that good would inevitably turn into evil and evil into good with the passage of years. We rejected the war between good and evil. We would fight it no more. Villains were made villains by circumstances, and we must fight the circumstances, not the poor individual wretches whose antisocial actions caused trouble. Peace conferences were held and humane agreements concerning the usages of war were made among the nations. Naval strength was adjusted by treaty, and battleships were sunk to limit the power of those who had too much. It was an era of reason and good feeling that seemed destined to last interminably. Having emerged into sunlight out of the darkness of history, we saw our way clearly. We saw clearly in those high-minded times that the race was not going to live by the Old or the New Testament. It was going to live in the light of scientific day, making its choices freely among the fruits of the new trees of knowledge. Crime was a disease, and curable. Poverty was a disease, and curable. God was to be replaced by a sort of higher expedience, arrived at by laboratory methods. There was no sin except that which made for inefficiency. Honor was a hold-over from the past, retained mainly for business reasons. The need for sexual restraint was abolished by the discovery of contraceptives. Men were like trees, the race was like a forest. They needed nothing except proper conditions and free functioning to grow and prosper as never before. If there had been scarcities, if men had lacked and suffered, all lacks could be supplied by the multiplication of machinery. If there had been grim and terrible feuds over the love of a woman, the ownership of land or the conflicts of worship, they had become laughably unnecessary. Love should be free, land should bear beyond the capacity of the race to consume, religion was a laid ghost. We were to go forward and eat and drink and be merry, and right and wrong would dissolve into a series of realistic choices between that which was healthful and that which was poisonous.

Since every man's thinking is directed or deflected by that of his age, we all of us, in the nineteen-twenties, stared hard at this new and dazzling age which we were assured was just beyond the next elections. To most people it was not only acceptable but welcome as an inevitable step forward. What kind of environment it would make for us if it came, none of us knew. What dangers lurked under its shiny blessings, we could only guess. There was no precedent for the utopia of invention. Men were mainly concerned, then, as always, with the problem of keeping some kind of place for themselves, philosophically and economically, on this whirling ball. It was no longer expected that the gods would help us. We knew no gods and honored no decalogue. We had a low opinion of the race of men and therefore of ourselves.

Yet it was in these godless nineteen-twenties that I stumbled upon the only religion I have. And I came upon it in the most unlikely and supposedly godless of places. I was a journalist, and I knew nothing about the theatre except casually from the outside. But I wrote a verse tragedy, being bored with writing editorials, and a gallant producer put it on the stage – for no reason that I can see now. It failed quietly, as it deserved, but after its production the theatre tugged at me, its rewards dazzled me – and I wrote other plays, some of them successful. However, from the very beginning the theatre was to me, in some fundamental ways, an exasperating puzzle. Some plays succeeded, some did not, and why, nobody knew. Success on the stage seemed to be one of the ultimate mysteries. Leaving aside the questions of acting and directing, the problems of theme, story and writing appeared only more confused when discussed by the professors of playwriting. I developed a theory, which still looks cogent to me, that a playwright's first success was always largely accidental. After that he could analyze what he had done – and begin to develop an intuition that would take him through the maze of difficulties and dangers his action and dialogues must thread. But intuition is an unreliable guide, and I was not as intuitive as some others. I needed a compass – or a pole star – or some theory of what the theatre was about, and I had none.

However, I did discover that there were rules of playwriting which could not be broken. One by one I unearthed them for myself, or dug them out of the treatises of predecessors. And by and by some of them began to look like essentials. Let me cite a few of the first that come clear to me.

(1) The story of a play must be the story of what happens within the mind or heart of a man or woman. It cannot deal primarily with external events.

The external events are only symbolic of what goes on within.

(2) The story of a play must be a conflict – and specifically, a conflict between the forces of good and evil within a single person. The good and evil to be defined, of course, as the audience wants to see them.

(3) The protagonist of a play must represent the forces of good and must win, or, if he has been evil, must yield to the forces of the good, and know himself defeated.

(4) The protagonist of a play cannot be a perfect person. If he were he could not improve, and he must come out at the end of the play a more admirable human being than he went in.

When I had once begun to make discoveries of this sort, they came thick and fast. And they applied, not, as is natural to suppose, to extraordinary plays only – to Shakespeare and Jonson and the Greeks – but to all plays, and to those in our modern repertory as much as any others. I add a few more of the ancient and inescapable rules as they come to me.

(5) The protagonist of a play must be an exceptional person. He or she cannot be run-of-the-mill. The man in the street simply will not do as the hero of a play. If a man be picked from the street to occupy the center of your stage, he must be so presented as to epitomize qualities which the audience can admire. Or he must indicate how admirable human qualities can be wasted or perverted – must define an ideal by falling short of it, or become symbolic of a whole class of men who are blocked by circumstances from achieving excellence in their lives.

(6) Excellence on the stage is always moral excellence. A struggle on the part of a hero to better his material circumstances is of no interest in a play unless his character is somehow tried in the fire, and unless he comes out of his trial a better man.

(7) The moral atmosphere of a play must be healthy. An audience will not endure the triumph of evil on the stage.

(8) There are human qualities for which the race has a special liking on the stage: in a man, positive character, strength of conviction not shaken by opposition; in a woman, fidelity, passionate faith. There are qualities which are especially disliked on the stage: in a man, cowardice, any refusal to fight for a belief; in a woman, an inclination toward the Cressid.

These are precepts, of course, only for the writing of a play. The presentation is quite as important, and hedged about with as many commandments; but since I am neither actor nor director I am aware of only a few. Let me indicate what some of them are. When you choose an actor to play the leading role in a play you try to find a man who is not only a good actor, but who can be looked upon with admiration by the people out in front. This may seem simple enough to do, but it is not. When you are casting a play you become acutely conscious of the mental, physical and moral shortcomings of the human race. If you will stand in the lobby of a theatre as the patrons come in and examine them with the idea of finding a man or a woman who could take a leading part in the play, you will be disconcerted by the imperfection of mankind. So few, so lamentably few, would stand the test of the center of the stage, the concentrated lights and the concentrated scrutiny of a thousand fellow creatures insistent on perfection, or an approach to perfection. In that pool of light at the center of the stage all defects are magnified. Pick out the handsome, the attractive, the beautiful, the youthfully engaging and let the dissecting stares play on them one by one. Suppose you have chosen the best out of thousands. Suppose they are all attractive at first glance; but look again, for the audience will look again. Perhaps you find a too heavy jaw, slightly thin nostrils, an inadequate forehead, a shifty eye, faintly clumsy legs, an awkward pose, over-eagerness, timidity, a slight indication of grossness, illness, hesitant speech. Physical defects are less disastrous than mental or spiritual faults. One in ten thousand will be worthy to stand in that blaze, and like as not that one, even if he be an actor, is a bad one, tied up emotionally, unable to pour his soul into words and emotional states not his own.

I list these technical difficulties because they began eventually to have one meaning for me. They mean that the purpose of the theatre is to find, and hold up to our regard, what is admirable in the human race. The theatrical profession may protest as much as it likes, the theologians may protest, and the majority of those who see our plays would probably be amazed to hear it, but the theatre is a religious institution devoted entirely to the exaltation of the spirit of man. It has no formal religion. I am only trying now to arrive at what that religion is, but there is no doubt in my mind that our theatre, instead of being, as the evangelical ministers used to believe, the gateway to hell, is as much of a worship as the theatre of the Greeks, and has exactly the same meaning in our lives.

When I first wrote plays this statement would have seemed incredible to me. Broadway in the twenties, in the thirties, and now in 1941, has always worn an air of hard, garish, cheap professionalism. The lights, the chilly box-office men, the ornate and dirty buildings, the groups of actors lingering in drug-stores and along side streets, these all proclaim clearly a place of entertainment for sale. The priests and priestesses of these temples are certainly unaware of the nature of their profession. But consider what they sell, and you face a different prospect. The plays that please most and run longest in these sin-haunted alleys are representative of human loyalty, courage, love that purges the soul, grief that ennobles. Sometimes a simple tale like *Victoria Regina*, the story of a young girl faced suddenly with the responsibilities of an empire, unequal at first to the task, but developing and learning with the years, acquiring tolerance, wisdom and dignity, dying a great queen. Perhaps the story of Abraham Lincoln, a man with great endowments but afraid of life, forcing himself to face life, forcing himself to lead a nation in a war that sickened his soul, emerging at the end a great man. For those to whom this theory is novel it will seem easy to refute. The case of *Rain* will come up, where the uncritical tolerance and good will of a prostitute are held better moral guides than the fanatical zeal of the missionary.

They are better moral guides, no doubt of it. But the play does not praise the woman for being a prostitute. It finds virtue in her despite her vocation. It does not condemn the man for his religion, but for the perversion of religion into an evil force. The case of *Tobacco Road* will come up, in which a poor white family struggles with a burden of poverty, ignorance and adverse social conditions. There is no doubt that the run of the play was stimulated by a morbid curiosity concerning the unashamed sexual customs of the inhabitants of that mythical road through the tobacco fields, but if there had been no moral values in the piece nobody would have cared to see it. The sexual customs or lack of them wouldn't have drawn a nickel. There were heroic qualities in Jeeter Lester and his strange brood. They lacked many virtues. They were shiftless, dishonest, financially hopeless. But they were not afraid. They faced existence as it was handed out to them in a way that made them both pathetic and tragic. Nothing better is expected of any hero on the stage than this – that he take up what arms he has against what enemies assail him and come out of the battle with his morale intact. Jeeter Lester kept very little except his self-respect, but he did keep that, and those who saw him had a respect both for him and for the human spirit that cannot be quenched by squalor. I have witnessed several plays on Broadway that attempted to imitate *Tobacco Road* by duplicating the adverse conditions and the resultant twisted lives and depressed morals. But they were failures because they assumed that the public wanted only dirt. It wasn't the dirt of *Tobacco Road* that give it a long run, but the accompanying, and to many invisible, gallantry of its people.

Perhaps I have made my point nauseatingly clear, but I should like to present a little more evidence. As everybody knows, the great plays of the world – those accepted by civilization as part of a great heritage and played for centuries – these are almost all concerned with the conduct of exceptional men or women in positions of great responsibility, men with tragic faults and weaknesses but with mind and strength enough to overcome in the struggle with evil forces, both those within themselves and those without. This is *Hamlet*, *The Cid*, *Prometheus*. And it is also, please note, *Abe Lincoln in Illinois*. In such cases it is obvious that some kind of religious ritual is involved in reviving these symbols of national or cultural faith in a public performance. The *Oresteia* of Aeschylus is a ritual of crime and punishment, and ends by stating that Zeus himself must grow and learn and change if he is to avoid injustice. But here again we have a modern instance. *The Green Pastures* treats exactly the same theme, God's justice, and ends with exactly the same lesson, that God must learn and grow and change or his rigid justice will become an injustice in the end. I am fairly certain that Marc Connelly did not intentionally preach from the text of Aeschylus, but his play is no less a religious observance because it was presented in a plush-chaired theatre off our own gaudy Broadway. The worshippers pay a fairly high rent for their pews in the theatrical Forties, and not many of them realize that they are assisting in a worship, but they sit in church nevertheless, and acquire virtue thereby according to their understanding and the wisdom and skill of the functioning playwright. *Oedipus Tyrannus* and *Macbeth* and *Little Eyolf* and *The Little Foxes* teach one and all that an evil action revenges itself upon the doer. *Antigone* and *Hamlet* and ten thousand modern plays argue that injustice is a corrosive, and will eat the heart out of him who practices it. Analyze any play you please which has survived the test of continued favor, and you will find a moral or a rule of social conduct or a rule of thumb which the race has considered valuable enough to learn and pass along. Take such seemingly meaningless escapades as *You Can't Take It with You* and *The Time of Your Life*. The first says simply that money isn't everything, and the second says, as plainly as the author can speak, that tolerance is the great virtue. These are platitudes, of course. A play is not required to make ethical discoveries. It is only required to have a meaning, and a sound one – one, that is, which is accepted as sound by its audience. Put on a play which sets out to prove that dishonesty is the best policy and vice is triumphant in human affairs, and the audience will refuse it coldly. They don't want to believe it and they won't. You can poke farcical fun at homicide, as in *Arsenic and Old Lace* or *The Playboy of the Western World* or *The Beggar's Opera*, but you can not seriously praise an unrepentant murderer. The race – or the audiences – will not allow it. They will register disapproval and they will stay away.

There have been critics who held that the theatre was central among the arts because it is a synthesis of all of them. Now I confess that the theatre appears to me to be the central art – but for a different reason. It does bring together all the arts, or a number of them. But its distinction is that it brings them together in a communal religious service. Any other art, practiced separately, can be either moral or amoral, religious or pagan, affirmative or despairing. But when they come together in the theatre they must affirm, they can not deny. It is as if poetry, music, narration, dancing and the mimetic arts were bits and pieces of theatrical art, stripped away to function alone, and rudderless without the moral compulsion of the theatre.

And now I must give a definition of what seems to me morally sound. If an artist believes that there is good and that there is evil, and in his work favors what seems to him good, and expects ultimate victory for it, then he is morally sound. If he does not believe in the existence of good and evil, or if, believing in them, he asks, or even anticipates, the triumph of evil, he is morally unsound. To some artists the present good may seem evil and the present evil good. That has happened often in the case of a poet or a prophet. A playwright can not run so far ahead of his audience, for he must find a common denominator of belief in his own generation, and even the greatest, the loftiest, must say something which his age can understand.

In brief, I have found my religion in the theatre, where I least expected to find it, and where few will credit that it exists. But it is there, and any man among you who tries to write plays will find himself serving it, if only because he can succeed in no other way. He will discover, if he works through his apprenticeship, that the theatre is the central artistic symbol of the struggle of good and evil within men. Its teaching is that the struggle is eternal and unremitting, that the forces which tend to drag men down are always present, always ready to attack, that the forces which make for good can not sleep through a night without danger. It denies the doctrine of the nineteen-twenties emphatically. It denies that good and evil are obverse and reverse of the same coin, denies that good can win by waiting. It denies that wars are useless and that honor is without meaning. It denies that we can live by the laboratory and without virtue. It affirms that the good and evil in man are the good and evil of evolution, that men have within themselves the beasts from which they descend and the god toward which they climb. It affirms that evil is what takes man back toward the beast, that good is what urges him up toward the god. It affirms that these struggles of the spirit are enacted in the historic struggles of men – some representing evil, some good. It offers us criteria for deciding what is good and what is evil. Set a man on the stage and you know instantly where he stands morally with the race. Set Hitler on the stage and loathing will rise from every seat in the house. Even in Germany, if he were a character in a play, he would be hated and despised. Even in Germany, you can not be pitiless, merciless, ruthless, arrogant and without God on the stage, and be considered a hero. Let the author of *The Wave of the Future* be warned; let Mr. Lindbergh and Senator Wheeler be warned; that which is considered despicable on the stage will be held despicable in real life – not only evil but those who will not fight evil are hated on the stage. A man who accepts the wave of the future and analyzes honor to a breath can be the comedian to be laughed at but he can not be the protagonist. According to the worshippers of the good who sit in our theatres a hero may have his doubts and indecisions, for that's only human, but when it comes to the test he must be willing to take steel in his bosom or take lead through his intestines or he resigns his position as a man. The audience, sitting in our theatres, makes these rules and, in setting them, defines the purposes and beliefs of *homo sapiens*. There is no comparable test that I know of for what is good in the human soul, what is most likely to lead to that distant and secret destination which the race has chosen for itself and will somehow find.

The Basis of Artistic Creation in Music

ROY HARRIS

THE basis of artistic creation in music can only be found in humanity itself. From this source has arisen all creative impulses. From humanity has flowed forth a never ending stream of creative vitality, slowly shaping from the dark, vague recesses of his inner self, our human world – our idioms of thought, our symbols and all equipment which has ever been used or ever will be used in the complex process of daily living.

Throughout the groping search for a way of living, man has been driven and guided by a gnawing hunger for satisfaction. And this need for satisfaction has been exceedingly elusive. Born from within man, it has always seemed to entice him from just beyond the horizons of his experience. Of man, it was always beyond him. This elusive, ever present need for satisfaction would not permit man to accept the bare necessities of physical existence as an ultimate objective. His food must not only fill his stomach and strengthen his blood, it must satisfy his ever changing sense of taste. His shelter, his domestic surroundings, his instruments of war and symbols of worship must not only be serviceable; they must satisfy his ever changing sense of proportion, texture, color. When he was not hunting, eating, sleeping, or making war, unused time beckoned his need for satisfaction to a ceaseless exploration of himself and his environment. Time opened the door to his craving need for the satisfaction of new experience. On and on, man has led himself in his search for the satisfying interests of an ever-expanding, ever-more-complex world of perception – always leading to new conceptions from within himself.

Half-mad with discontent, half-ecstatic with joyous discovery, he has gropingly created always in his own image. He has created polytheistic gods and monotheistic gods, all superlatively endowed with his own most desirable attributes. From his minute examination of himself and his environment, he has created systems of thought, of trade and commerce, of government. He has created the arts and sciences and crystallized all of them into tradition; to which he in turn has passionately avowed undying allegiance, until he himself created new pathways toward those horizons to which time forever lures him.

From the early stages of man's never-ending search for satisfaction, he has been preoccupied with the hypnotic effect that sound has had on him. He discovered that the impact of sound upon his eardrums when reiterated in rhythmic patterns could arouse him to intense states of emotional excitement. He gradually realized that these states of emotional excitement lifted him into a new world – an intense, absorbing, hypnotic world exclusively of his own making. In this new, intangible world, he could contemplate his past, his present, the future.

With sound, he could recall the emotional states of great moments in his past experience – he could intensify the most important aspects of his immediate life and project himself into the hoped-for future by inducing with sound those emotional states which most satisfied him.

Moreover, by repeatedly experiencing these emotional states, he could arouse his generative active self with increasing ease and effectiveness. He gained an ever-increasing control over the emotive power-house within himself. His will to act was stimulated by intense emotional experience. Here was a strange persuasive language which simultaneously aroused and liberated his deepest, most vague impulses – his sleeping emotions.

With sound, he could lash himself into a frenzy of courage which gloried in battle, into a sweet melancholy of self-abnegation worthy of the most awesome suppliance to his gods, into such festive earth moods that his very blood became the wine of pantheistic delight.

Man's use of sound has grown in subtlety and complexity as man himself has become increasingly subtle and complex in his mind and emotions.

In the beginning, he was intoxicated with the reiteration of percussive rhythmic designs on monotone instruments. If the rhythmic pulse was faster than the heart-beat, it tended to excite the emotions which generate physical activity; if the rhythmic pulse was slower than the heart-beat it tended to excite the emotions which generate contemplative introspection. Beyond this barbaric use of sound was discovered a new enchantment. Through centuries of groping experience, man gradually found within himself the lithe, supple power of melody. To rhythmic designs were added variable pitch designs, multiplying the subtleties of sound beyond computation, adding a new variation of expressiveness, identifying and distilling old experiences. A new world of instruments was invented to glorify man's hopes and fears, his victories and defeats, his elations and despairs – instruments of great variation in pitch and dynamics, instruments for all occasions. They were sounded together and with human voices – male and female, young and old – and harmony evolved.

A second new element of expressiveness – a new resonance of sound – an undreamed-of eloquence of inflection – was found. The harmonies were of bright or dark or pastel intensities. If they were bright, they elated man as the rising sun; if they were of pastel shades, they solaced him as the sweet calm of eventide; if they were dark, his emotions were plunged into the depths of bereaved solitude. Melodies began to absorb the moods of harmonies, and to make harmonies themselves as they sang their own way in complex designs against each other. More new instruments were invented by the fancy of man's search for himself. Instruments to intone melody and harmony more accurately, to sing the ever-changing world of man's making with virtuosic facility. And so, as the very shadow of man within him and beyond him, the use of sound has grown with man into the language of music. It has survived civilizations – with all their glories and tribulations, their political, economic, religious systems, their wars and pestilences, their changing blood-streams. All these mankind has survived and as part of man, music has survived also – always changing and evolving as man has changed and evolved.

Sound that began as the savage beating on a stretched skin over a hollowed tree has grown to music as we know it today. Music that grew in service to the communal institutions of man has become a communal institution itself. Music which served the ritualistic needs of a small tribe of superstitious savages now unites humanity at large in contemplation of man's highest, best and most intense emotional qualities.

In defiance of time and space, millions of men set aside an appointed hour to contemplate silently their inner being as aroused and liberated by the language of music, eloquently intoned by great orchestras of specialized musicians.

As music grows in the magnitude of its use and the eloquence of its utterance, we become increasingly aware that it is a uniquely human language. It increasingly enables humanity to escape the limitations of finite experience, and to live in the vast realm of the ever-shifting subconscious.

As radio and recording facilities daily become a more practical and direct means of interhuman communication, we are beginning to realize that even the word language itself depends largely for its meaning on the dynamic inflections of pitch and the tempo of rhythmic designs arising out of word combinations. Radio and recording facilities are swiftly conditioning man's aural apparatus and brain responses to a keener, more explicit understanding of the language of music and its subsidiary channels of sound effects.

It is understandable, then, that humanity should be concerned about the nature of this sound language – its characteristics, its properties, from where it comes, how it can be more fully comprehended, induced, and controlled.

What is the basis for creation in music? Music as we know it today is volatile, tonal architecture. It fills space with tonal volumes; it flows with time in rhythmic pulses. Its tonal volumes constantly change in magnitude, shape and texture. Its very continuity depends on the flow of its rhythmic pulses which carry it forward in time sequence. It is a time-space language, which, like time itself, can not be frozen into a static condition. Music can only exist in the time stream of its continuity. It can not be concrete. It is abstract.

The ever-shifting magnitudes of its volumes are determined by pitch relations; the mood-color and density of those volumes are determined by harmony, dynamics and orchestration. Its flow of continuity in time is determined by rhythmic pulse. The elusive volatility of music is its most salient characteristic, created of man, by man, for man, as a culture concentrate of his own deepest, most intense emotional experience.

Broadly stated, the basis for this uniquely human language is humanity itself. But if we wish to know more in detail about the language of music, we must consider its generative source and the ways and means mankind has invented to capture musical impulses into permanent translatable symbols.

All music has been created by individuals. Each part of every rhythmic design, every melodic contour, every harmonic cadence, every contrapuntal device, every form sequence, every instrument, all notation, was conceived once by an individual.

In the creative processes of these men, who as individuals have created and will continue to create music, we will find the basis of creation in music. What do they perceive which stimulates them to creative musical conception?

Psychology advises us that all conceptions are the result of the combining of two or more perceptions in the brain of the creative person. Psychology also advises other pertinent conclusions – that the focused attention necessary to keen perceptions cannot be achieved unless the individual is deeply interested in the object or state of being perceived, that some individuals have unusual powers of uniting perceptions into conceptions, and that these powers tend to be specialized according to specialized interests of perception.

All these processes are inextricably interwoven with the sensory equipment which the individual inherited, and the conditioning of that sensory equipment by his environment.

The composer, whose whole life is to be absorbed in a language of sound, must be born with the capacity for sensitive and intense aural perception, and his environment must condition his aural capacities toward creative ends. And since the language of music deals with man's emotions, the composer must be born and conditioned to possess an intense field of emotional activity and the powers to focus and translate that emotional activity whenever it occurs, either in himself, in individuals around him – or more abstrusely, in unconscious mass social fermentations.

The development of an emotional field of activity within himself and the capacity to perceive it within himself and around himself is perhaps the more important half of the creative musician's life-work. The other very difficult part is that of learning and mastering the use of an adequate musical vocabulary with which to translate his musical conceptions into traditional symbols which are serviceable to the musical world.

The creative musician, then, must conceive and translate. His world is dualistic. He must be able to live and grow in an acutely focused, *subjective* world arising out of an intense emotional field of activity. At the same time he must be so stimulated by this world that he naturally possesses a sustained interest strong enough to impel and guide him through a lifetime of searching for an adequate musical vocabulary, with which to objectify his subjective impulses in translatable traditional symbols.

From the very beginning the composer's life must be both subjective and objective. It is within these two processes of the creative musician that we will find the basis for creation in music. The basis for the subjective process is to be found in the individual's inherited field of emotions, and these are atavistic rather than parental. Our strongest emotions are bred into us from centuries of our striving ancestors. Their essential character cannot be changed, but they can be intensified and clarified through experience and learning. The actions which they generate can be guided and controlled. And this is the life-work of the creative musician.

With a given gamut and intensity of emotional activity which he inherited from countless generations of ancestors, he must conceive musical ideas and translate them into traditional symbols. His cultural environment will largely determine the idioms and even the natural trend of his musical ideas. They may be rhythmic, melodic or harmonic, contrapuntal, or even purely orchestral in nature. Whatever his spontaneous musical ideas may be, he must become aware of them and their characteristics. Then he must find the ways and means of formulating them.

In this process, the composer must accept the symbols of tradition. And this is good, because one generation is not long enough to invent a new language of symbols with which to formulate new personalized conceptions. Moreover, because the inherited, innate emotional field of the composer is atavistic, the symbols of his forefathers have been generated from emotions similar to those by which he, himself, is impelled. The symbols of tradition are therefore indispensable. Yet in each generation the composer is driven from within by his own ideas and from without by the dictates of his inarticulate social environment to formulate new idioms of expression which modify tradition and add to it.

In a sense, the history of musical development has been an incessant friction between the crystallized idioms of tradition and the modifications and additions of contemporary creators. At the time of their invention, these modifications and additions seem antithetical to the stream of musical development and are considered iconoclastic. Actually the sum total of these modifications of and additions to tradition constitute the body of tradition itself. The ceaseless trickle of individual conceptions adding to the traditional stream of music has been cumulative through the centuries. Together, creative individuals have created music as surely as springs and tributaries have gathered into the seaward rivers.

The subjective processes of perception and conception as well as the objective processes of technical notation, as practiced by living musicians, constitute the basis of artistic creation in music.

As singers of inarticulate humanity, creative musicians have been the living embodiment of the basis for creation in music. Through them has flowed the emotional experience of their progenitors. By them, those uniquely human attributes are intensified, reaffirmed, released and translated into serviceable idioms of culture. Innately of the past, reflecting the present, they in turn modify the future.

Born in the present of the strongest physical and emotional rootstocks of the past, creative musicians live to record the emotional gamut and intensities of society in the economic, social and educational fermentations of today. With their own modifications of the traditionalized symbols of our forefathers, they preserve the spirit of these symbols.

As the living affirmation of man's faith in himself, they embody the basis for artistic creation in music, in the ever-present Now. To indict them is to indict the society which bore and fertilized them. To expect eloquent utterance from them is to embrace the society which we create by our daily living actions.

The Basis of Artistic Creation in the Fine Arts

RHYS CARPENTER

THE ARTIST'S greatest and most necessary illusion is the illusion that he is creating. Rob him of that belief and you have shorn him of his power. It is his Samson's hair, his witch's mouse, his giant's girdle, the source of all his strength. Fortunately for him, he will not admit to anyone that the creative power within him, on which he so utterly depends, can be illusory, since he has the most direct and convincing counter-evidence within his own experience as an artist. Who gives the formless clay its shape, if not the man whose hand fashions it? Out of the meaningless block of marble emerges whatever image the sculptor envisages and desires. What fuller freedom could there be than that vouchsafed by a blank canvas and unsqueezed tubes of paint? Out of materials which – artistically – are nothing at all, the artist creates the work of art, to exercise his own volition and to match his own imaginings. With such immediate evidence before him, it is not likely that he will lose his belief in the reality of the creative act.

Yet the artist's confidence in his own unlimited power to create is fallacious. Though false, it is necessary; for if he loses this illusion, he can no longer act. Yet even in his action the critical onlooker can see that the sense of freedom is deceptive. For otherwise, how is it that to the trained beholder every painting proclaims not merely its maker, but also its date and its environment? If the artist were wholly free to create, why should not each of his creations be completely unique, instead of showing a manner appropriate to a school or group, which in turn takes its ordered place within a phase or style pointing back to its predecessors and forward toward its successors? Even El Greco and Van Gogh, however erratically different from their contemporaries, fit intimately their particular time and place within the evolution of painting. It is of course the old dilemma of the freedom of the human will: we may act freely according to our judgment, choice, and desires; but our judgment, choice, and desires themselves are motivated and conditioned by our own past and by the present world surrounding us.

This universal human condition certainly jeopardizes the artist's claim to independence, and suggests at the least a certain tyranny of styles and fashions which he must follow and placate in order to succeed. Such styles and fashions, moreover, are more exacting than the mere whims which seem to dictate our ordinary life in the shifting irrelevancy of dress and clothing, pastime and fads. We do not date paintings as we assign the correct year to a stray plate from Godey's *Lady's Book*. True, the history of Spanish court dress will be reflected in Velasquez' portraits and thus will date them; and the shifting architectural styles of Gothic and Renaissance may be discovered in the background scaffolding of many a European painting and so betray the time of their creation; but we do not mean that a canvas is thus dated by its imitation of contemporary objects amid its pictured contents. Works of art are stamped, through and through, over and over, with their specific phase in the long evolution of technical style.

I have failed in my argument if I do not make it clear what I mean by style. Let me rather arbitrarily insist that style and manner are to be distinguished as day from night. Every artist will have a manner, which is merely an indication that no two human individuals are alike in anything they do and that all our activity is based on routine repetition and habit and so falls into a characteristic pattern. To acquire technical competence is to form a manner. But style transcends the individual, even though the individual may by his manner contribute to form a style. Style is all that structure and articulation by which a painted picture or a carved marble becomes emotionally intelligible. And, being this, style is not at the individual artist's discretion nor created at his command. Let us not boggle over verbal definitions: if this is not what you mean by style, then give it some other name. But let us recognize that there is something which guides and shapes the destiny of artistic expression through the generations and centuries, something neither wilful nor chaotic, but ordered, measured, and inexorable. This something shows itself most clearly as a technical evolution; its distinguishable phases I am calling style.

That which appears to the casual onlooker as a welter

of disconnected individual effort, whose record possesses as little internal coherence as the schoolboy's chronicle of battles, conquerors, and kings, becomes for the properly trained art-historian a biological process with a teleological trend. As such, it transcends any given individual by a huge span of time. The task which confronts the mimetic artist who strives to reproduce forms of the real world in pigments or clay or stone or metal is so formidable that no civilization in the world's history has produced a realistically illusionary painting or a correctly articulated human statue in less than five hundred years of effort. Thus, the classical world took six centuries to reach its most realistic stage in sculpture, China took nearly a thousand years, Western Europe (like Greece) about six hundred; while classical painting evolved to illusionistic realism through eight centuries, and modern European through six. Subordinated to such processes, no single artist has ever been responsible for more than a contributory impulse to his art. The great movements which so generously overlap the span of his own lifetime are stronger and more vital than he. The individual artist attains his own status by submission to the contemporary trend. There is no contradiction in adding that such submission normally involves revolt against a preceding phase. As in the weird priesthood of Diana on the shores of Lake Nemi, where the new servant of the goddess must slay his predecessor and in the end himself be slain, the artist who dominates his generation rises by his own revolt and is superseded by another's, yet carries onward all the while the continuous service of a single craft.

The extent to which the artist is dependent on the technical evolution of his medium is by now a commonplace to the art-historian, but still rather generally treated with scepticism by the layman, who shares the artist's own illusion of complete creative autonomy. Actually, artistic morphology is a perfectly straightforward topic of investigation, study, and instruction. But unfortunately for our immediate purpose here, it rather resembles the geometrical propositions of Euclid which so vexed the Alexandrian Ptolemy because he could not grasp them all in a single lecture. Yet it deals with very downright and familiar topics, such as perspective, vanishing-points, illusion of space and distance, atmospheric gradations of color, foreshortening, cast shadows, illumination, plastic suggestion – in short, all matters geometrical, physical, and optical which beset and perplex the practitioner anxious to set upon canvas an adequately illusionary presentation of the sunlit outside world of sight. So great are these perplexities, so slow and intricate the resolution of their manifold conflicting problems and – a most vital point – so hierarchic is their marshalling into an ordered sequence, with certain phases necessarily ordained to belong to the early periods, others to the middle epochs, still others to the culminating maturity of technique, that the whole history of painting in modern Europe since Duccio has had to fit itself into the framework of this long and virtually uninterrupted progress, which I shall call the Great Tradition.

There is abundant testimony that the leading painters and sculptors of the past, in despite of all self-centered illusion of omnipotence engendered by their creative activities, have been so engrossed in technical problems as to feel at times uncertain in their minds whether craftsmanship might not be their truest leader and prime helper. Leonardo da Vinci, Duerer, nineteenth century French landscape painters – to choose only a few out of a great company – certainly devoted a large part of their time and energy to exploring and exploiting technical resources. We of today have little realization of the amount of labor expended on the long road from apprenticeship to mastery, whereon the world's artists have all had to travel in the past. The popular notion of genius, surviving probably from the Romantic movement, as an effortless and God-given illumination, descending like the Pentecostal dove on the chosen few, has corrupted our understanding of the artist's real nature and encouraged all manner of outrage, ranging from laziness to sheer impudence, in the self-chosen apostle of today, who has indeed a gift of tongue, but no other manifestation of divinity. Until recently, art has been very hard work. It still is so for those who preserve any continuity with the Great Tradition.

There is submission, obedience, and discipline in the acquirement of any technically difficult accomplishment. But when that accomplishment is not solely a display of dexterity, like balancing one billiard ball on top of another, but is a living part of a human process involving generations of practitioners, then tyranny becomes transmuted into a service of perfect freedom. Out of this absorbed submission to the dictates of technical attainment has been bred the distinctive manner, the poignant power, the brilliance and enthusiasm of the great artists. Take away from Signorelli his delight in rendering the modelled nude with all its muscles shown in superficial action, take away from Mantegna his comprehension of the correct geometric solution of extreme foreshortening, take away from Rembrandt the device of showing illumination amid enveloping darkness, and you would have utterly lamed these artists in their stride. Yet teach a modern student to model like Signorelli, foreshorten like Mantegna, envelop like Rembrandt, and nothing of importance will result. Why? For a very simple reason. Signorelli, Mantegna, Rembrandt were excitedly discovering the technical resources on which they laid such emphasis; and for an artist thus absorbed and involved, there will be no distinction (such as the schoolmen draw) between discovery, invention, and creation. Signorelli must have felt that he was himself creating the device of sculptural modelling in paint; Mantegna may well have thought that he had invented certain extreme devices of foreshortening; Rembrandt must have been convinced that he himself had discovered a new painter's world of light amid darkness. And thus it was possible for these coldly academic matters of technique to convert themselves into flaming emotional resources by which craftsmen were transmuted into master artists.

And now, in the twentieth century after Christ, after some six hundred years of energetic life, the Great Tradition has reached its close. The ancient Etruscan soothsayers taught that there were mighty revolutions and changes occurring in appointed cycles of time. "And when one age is run out, at the approach of another, there appears some wonderful sign from earth or heaven, such as makes it manifest at once to those who have made it their business to study such things, that there has succeeded in the world a new race of men, with new customs and new institutions." Art's epochal cycles too have their omens and portents, their doleful blasts of trumpets in the unclouded sky. The ending of the Great Tradition was first presaged a full hundred years before its occurrence. Wherever the technical trend is toward illusionistic realism (as in West European art), the first token of imminent dissolution is classicism, the second is archaisticism, the third and last is universal eclecticism. These are the trumpets blowing in the sky. To the Great Tradition of our modern world, classicism came at the close of the eighteenth century with such figures as Canova and Thorwaldsen in sculpture, Louis David and a little later Ingres in painting. The second trumpet blew when the Pre-Raphaelite Brotherhood proclaimed its backward-gazing faith and there were Gothic and Romanesque and Byzantine revivals. The third trumpet, loudest and nearest, is even now still blowing in our ears. By calling it "universal eclecticism" I mean to characterize it as the restless seeking and casting-about for other ways and alien manners, whether early Greek or Italian primitive; Cambodian, West African, Mayan, Pacific; childish, negroid, ribald, lunatical; all in the expectation that these would bring some new sweet or savor to the palate jaded by the outworn flavor of the Great Tradition – itself so overwhelmingly greater than any of the petty tribes of the new fetishisms, Indian or negroid, arctic or equatorial.

At such a spectacle, there is no occasion for anger or for grief, since men should not rail at destiny, and this aversion from the Great Tradition was inevitable. Six hundred years of technical development – not always at a steady pace, but almost always in the same direction – had brought the cardinal problem of western painting as close to solution as the problem itself apparently permitted. That problem was a purely technical one, wholly contained within the medium of expression – to devise an accurate two-dimensional equivalent in terms of opaque pigments for the three-dimensional world of sunlit actuality. No one supposes that he is looking at the real world when he is looking at a painting, hence the illusion cannot be complete nor the likeness utterly exact. Nevertheless, when we observe, firstly, that a kodachrome film can not merely reproduce but can almost exactly duplicate a piece of painting, and, second, that the kodachrome picture is a two-dimensional colored representation of the outside world of our everyday experience employing essentially the same devices of perspective, foreshortening, illumination, tonal gradation of color, tactile and visual suggestion, which the academic realist painter uses, we are entitled to two conclusions: one, that kodachrome by purely mechanical means probably comes as near as is mechanically and physically possible to translating the solid sun-illumined world of normal vision into the flat intangible realm of pictorial illusion; the other, that the essential identity of the devices for making this transference by the impersonal camera and the highly personal artist is sufficient warrant that the technique of painting has likewise solved, up to the limit of its physical capacities, the major problems of sensuous suggestion. That is why the Great Tradition has ended: when it had solved all its puzzles and perfected all its technical devices, success left it nothing new to struggle for, or at any rate no obvious objective on which all men could agree. Up to a couple of generations ago, the technical problems involved in the art of painting were sufficiently clear and insistent to dictate to the practicing artist his general line of advance – and there is nothing more stimulating than to be told what to do, but to be left to find out for oneself how to do it! But by our own day and age, most of the problems had been correctly and hence finally solved and, with that, the obvious direction in which art was to move had ceased to be apparent.

There will be many who will judge so great an emphasis on the mere technical resources of art to be a mistake, believing quite rightly that the true fountain-head of all artistic activity must be the emotions and feelings rather than the exercise of that adroitness which attends the technical process and conditions its practical success. We value the great masters for something quite other than their facility. Art which does not have its source in emotion and does not find its end in a corresponding emotion in the beholder is mere academicism. True; but mere intensity of feeling never produced a work of art. I know no more abused or difficult problem in esthetic speculation than the essential difference between artistic emotion and ordinary everyday feelings. Beethoven senses the inexorability of Fate and so produces his fifth symphony; but what are the middle terms between a sense of helplessness in the hands of destiny, such as any of us may experience, and the opening bars of a musical passage such as none of us could compose? Let us grant that every artist must feel deeply and that without the deep stir of feeling his work can possess neither depth nor greatness. Yet it is not *because* he feels deeply that he can create greatly; nor are his feelings of any artistic moment as long as they remain within the bounds of everyday experience. Grief for mankind, or a high sense of human destiny, the gamut between exaltation and despair, are within the grasp of the unartistic; but only as they are transmuted into the specific forms of an artistic medium do such universal human emotions become artistically operative and communicable. I do not wish to labor an unnecessary point; but we must reject with the utmost conviction two widespread beliefs – one, that the artist has only to feel deeply in order to create; the other, that the emotions aroused by art are indistinguishable from the emotions which we experience in ordinary life. As long as we subscribe to this second fallacy we shall incline to demand from the artist the immediate reproduction of scenes in which such emotions are normally involved. The family physician at the bedside of the dying child can be faithfully pictured and will quite naturally awaken in the susceptibly minded an experience ripe for tears. It is precisely because this experience is not an artistic but a physically actual one, that the picture of the doctor at the bedside is not a work of art. At their most effective level, the arts do not illustrate or re-enact emotional situations, but evoke or impart more intimate and immediate emotional response through their own special channels. Clearly, it is not because he himself feels gloomy that the painter can paint a scene of brooding melancholy, but because he has adequately mastered a form of expression through which such a feeling can be suggested and conveyed. That is why I have laid such emphasis on technique and on the intense concentration of technical resources organized and vitalized into Style.

Whence comes this miraculous vitalizing power, which I have defined not as the artist's personal manner but as that broader discipline converting the layman's ordinary world of vision into the painted world of pigment, the cast world of bronze, the carved world of wood and stone? To answer that query is to say what and why art exists among men at all; but at least we can see that through the past six hundred years style has been so intimately conditioned by the artist's struggle with the technical problems of realistic representation that it is fair to say that the primary source of style has been technical vicissitude and resourcefulness. Style of this sort has grown and developed under physical compulsion: from painter to painter and sculptor to sculptor we can see it expand and unfold. Always its future has been implicit in its past, its past imminent in its present. Such style is self-evolved, dictated to the artist, who is himself engendered out of it. Within such fetters – as I have said again and again – moves, and has moved, the Great Tradition. And now that tradition has fulfilled itself by accomplishing its basic purpose, and has come to rest.

Just as there are only three ways of becoming rich – to inherit money, to borrow money, or to make money – so there are only three ways to attain an artistic style – to inherit it (as did all those who lived in the Great Tradition), to borrow it (as do those who imitate the artistic forms of civilizations other than their own), or lastly, to make it, to create a style (as we pray may in the end be vouchsafed to our modern world to do). I trust that you will not think it mere pedantry and love of pigeon-holing if I thus divide all styles into these three classes – the natural or evolved style, the borrowed or imitated style, and the independent or created style. And I hope that you will not judge the division drawn too arbitrarily, because so unevenly distributed in time, if I assign all West European painting from Giotto to Manet to Evolved Style, load the category of Borrowed Style with recent eclectic and imitative schools from Burne-Jones to the youthful Paul Manship, and claim all the weirdly heterogeneous phenomena of ultra-modern art, not for a new style, but for mere experimentation in search of such a new style.

Let me show you how this works out.

But first let us dispose of all merely borrowed styles, for I think that you will all agree with the findings.

What objection can be raised to so estimable a procedure as imitating excellence or adopting a good thing for one's own? If Greek and Chinese should chance to be judged man's highest achievement in sculpture and in painting respectively, why should not contemporary artists use the resources of such successful epochs? Were style nothing more than the individual's arbitrary and self-selected mode of expression, it might perhaps be possible to cast American art into Chinese or Hellenic patterns. I remind you in passing that there have been great classic revivals in Europe ere now. But precisely because style transcends the artists who use it, being itself a long-lived process, to transplant it is to kill it. The Pre-Raphaelites in the latter nineteenth century pretended to a restraint in foreshortening, spatial perspective, and *chiaroscuro* modelling which the Italian painters of the *quattrocento* did not feign and would gladly have overcome, had they known how. In sculpture, Canova and Thorwaldsen assumed a limitation on anatomical detail which the fifth century Greeks never assumed, but actually possessed, and could not immediately resolve. To adopt a primitive manner is not to attain a primitive artist's intensity of feeling or strength of technical resolution. If our contention is true that, although the emotion in painting is by no means merely the display of craftsmanship incident to surmounting technical difficulties, nonetheless it is through surmounting and therewith utilizing and exploiting the technical obstacles in their path that painters have been able to create forms of emotional expression, then we may be well convinced that artistic emotion emanates from style, and style derives from technical struggle and success. And the difference between true contest with its hard-earned victory and pretended strife with its fictitious and meretricious outcome will be the measure of the spiritual gulf between a true primitive and a neo-primitive master. The fetishes of the West African coastlands often show an uncontaminated purity of form which rightly makes them admirable for us today and earns them a place in our museums of art, not merely in our museums of ethnology; but just because their style is so self-centered, self-contained, and for a Negro culture so appropriate, it can not be grafted on our own utterly different civilization nor utilized for our own art. Every assumed or borrowed style is an evolutionary anachronism: being without life, it is without lasting value.

And thus it is that our artists of today, since they can not inherit a living style, the Great Tradition being ended, and must not borrow a style, are forced to invent one. That, for the past fifty years, they have been trying their best to do.

If you are at home in recent art history, you will know that the so-called "out-of-door" or *plein air* movement in late nineteenth century France was a technical advance which still was made under the impulse of the Great Tradition, because it sought to reproduce actual appearances more convincingly. To mere correctness of color-tone it sought to add the glitter of true sunlight, and to the even clarity and accuracy of represented objects it sought to apply the blur surrounding focal definition and attention. But when Seurat set little blobs of bright color side by side not merely to bring an illusion of strong outdoor illumination to his scene, but because he had discovered that he could achieve a wholly new type of picture with its own curious suggestion of everyday objects frozen and stiffened and glittering in a sort of carnival brilliance, then the search for a new style and the revolt against mimetic realism had in truth begun. This conversion of the luminous liquidity of the seen world into hard frozen globules of strong color could not fail to entice succeeding artists into laying ever greater emphasis on these globules until, in rapid but orderly magnification, the globule grew from a speck (*pointillisme*) to a patch (*tachisme*) and to other artists suggested the use of still larger areas and extended surfaces. At the last, the arbitrary geometrical shapes of flat color invaded the entire fabric of the picture with triangles and squares and lozenges and polygons so vagarious that only their sharp angles and edges still proclaimed them to belong primarily to the artist's brain rather than to the complex outer world of landscape composition or human figures. Thus, quite logically, but probably out of no better esthetic sense than the experimenting and exploring faculty of reason, were begotten the studied destructions of ocular appearances to which we usually give the over-precise name of cubism, although geometrically the term is too restricted.

Cubism, the geometrical disintegration of visual actuality, naturally begot futurism, the utter dissolution of intelligible form. Divorced from all objective coherence, the new free forms were arbitrarily reassembled to suggest an inactual world in terms of dislocated fragments of the real. But meanwhile, as futurism progressed to its own logical self-destruction, the actualities of normal vision had been so completely and thoroughly violated that much of the content of these distraught pictures had ceased to mimic appearances of the real world and had become visually so incomprehensible as to evoke in the spectator only a sense of meaningless shapes and patterns and lines. You will grant that it was no great creative step, betokening power neither of thought nor imagination, if painters now began to experiment deliberately with unrepresentative shapes and lines and patterns in order to discover what responses they harbored within themselves. Out of such raw esthetic experimentation arose our recent school of non-objective or "abstract" art.

Painters had ceased to be conscious artists and had become laboratory workers testing all emotional resources directly or indirectly involved in the technical performance of reproduction. What are the emotional values latent in geometrical appeal? in colored pattern? in kinetic suggestion? If the mere visual content of the picture, its grass and rocks and trees, its snow or surf or winding lane, can not completely explain the picture's magic as a work of art, something else must be lurking behind, operating through some pattern of the composition, some movement in its lines, some chromatic harmony in its use of color, some spatial lure in its perspective of distances. So the way lies open for experiment in the abstract, with pattern, kinetic line, chromatic harmony, spatial suggestion, in order to wrest from this hidden company of generic forms the secret of their contribution to paintings. Shapes which are not shapes of anything which we see around us; perspective suggestion which is not that of our ordinary spatial world; color groupings which do not come to the eye looking out at its everyday environment – could not these be made the resources of the creative painter? Must the artist always imitate the common outside world of sense? Can he not create a new world of his own, a new world for art?

With all due respect to those who honestly believe the answer to these questions to be *Yes*, may I venture to suggest that these always most interesting, stimulating, and often wholly sincere experiments in abstract pictorial resources have by now abundantly proved the correct answer to be *No*?

We can only be grateful for these experiments. The esthetician is beholden to them as practical tests which he is not technically and temperamentally fitted to perform. The public is beholden to them for their initiation into the formal mechanism behind the visible world. Above all, the present-day artists should be beholden to them as a great and valuable demonstration in certain fundamental propositions of their craft. Do not accuse us of being blind or superior or stupid when we ask the practitioners of abstract art to believe us when we tell them that they are behaving not as creative artists but as experimental scientists and that their relation to painting is not very different from the relation which grammarians, philologists, linguists, and students of the psychology of speech bear to the actual practice of literature.

Now it may seem a curious thing that literature as a human art seems to flourish best under a truly monstrous assumption of the vast importance of mankind in the universal scheme. It does this because it must have its familiar and instantly identifiable subject-matter, which for human readers must apparently be man. Rob literature of this reference to human experience, this deliberate and unbounded overrating of humanity, and it becomes mere *belles lettres*, whimsy, technical exercise, dull or pretentious or hollow. In much the same way, painting must be picture-making, must somehow suggest the normal world of ocular experience, attach its emotional appeal to the universal human world of mortal sense and sight. Unless it thus refers to the same world which the eye sees when it is not looking at pictures, it cuts itself off from human experience – an amputation seemingly too great to be survived. We must not argue this proposition philosophically in the hope of logical proof or disproof – in esthetic argumentation any outcome is, alas, possible with much show of reason – we must accept it empirically as the well-nigh unanimous finding of five thousand years of human activity in art. These sorrowful times should have taught us that our unparalleled success in mechanics, physics, and chemistry has not changed us into a new category of human being. In our morals, our feelings, our behavior, our practical wisdom, we have made no change and can prove no progress. Endowed with all our machinery and exploiting so marvellously the material resources of our planet, we are still no better and no different race from that unhappy species of *homo* so unwisely dubbed *sapiens*. It is idle to think that we can make for ourselves a fundamentally new and different kind of art unless we indeed believe that we have made of ourselves a fundamentally different kind of man.

Some such realization has everywhere of late been gaining ground. From the fascinating playing-field of cubism, futurism, and abstractionism the artists have begun to flock back to the everyday world of reality. During the past two decades the popularity of abstract art has waned and its output correspondingly diminished. Yet the consequent return to representation has left the problem almost precisely where it was. Only surrealism has offered a really new avenue of escape by applying the rehabilitated creed of objective accuracy not directly to the everyday world of sight but to that shattered and disintegrated world which impressionism and futurism and all their followers had produced. One could observe objective truth with all fidelity, yet alter the normal arrangements of objects in space, redistributing and recombining fragments of objective truth according to the dictates of the most wayward fancy. Surrealism maintains the visual objectivity of the world of sense, but destroys its structural laws and habitual behavior. It preserves the chance physical object, but severs its casual and geographical nexus with other objects. Instead of misrepresenting optical appearances, it mislocalizes them, thus creating a Behind-the-Looking-Glass Land where no photographer – hated virtuoso in effortless realism – no traditional painter, in the last analysis no other artist of any sort can follow. That such a dislocation of the divine ordering of this world has no counterpart outside the uniquely individual painting is no demerit, but an indication of its imaginative status. In our ordinary experience as human beings, the physical nexus which holds the world to its traditional pattern is thus visibly loosened for us only in our dreams, whence comes the easy (but probably fatal) connection of surrealism with Freudism.

I say "probably fatal" because we know both theoretically and by actual experience that there is a hierarchy to the esthetic emotions, that they extend upward into the spiritual realm as well as downward into the sensual, and that they do not persist at the level of immediate sensation. We know further that whimsy, the bizarre, the absurd, the irrational, the lecherous, are often highly diverting and attracting, yet are by their very nature debarred from the higher reaches of human feeling and can not come to even a glimpse of that "Love which moves the sun and th' other stars," with which Dante closes his poem of ascent into the heights. A painter reproducing everyone's everyday world may never lift it from the commonplace; but at least there exists the possibility of translating its banality to those emotional heights to which extraordinary men have now and again moved it. But the painter who destroys the world's coherence can never appeal to the universal, but only to the particular, *his* particular; for that the universal human world of the subconscious can be drawn up into the conscious world of illustration and objectively pictured, seems a direct contradiction in terms. At best, even if some suggestive evocation of such a world is possible, surrealism has handicapped itself by choosing a level of experience shared by distorting mirrors on amusement piers, dreams and nightmares, fantasy and fooling. We well may wish for painting a better future and a worthier fate.

But must that future be only the old and by now rather trite domain of objective realism?

That there has been a return to realism is certain; but whether the curiously stark regional self-consciousness, which marks much American painting of today, has been the occasion or the result of this return to realism would not be easy to discover. In either event, it is obvious that geographical and physical differences such as attend on a shift of scene from Kansas to Canada, from Mississippi to Minnesota, can be most easily expressed in realistically imitative terms. If it is the details which mark the differences and confer the local individuality of scene, then detail must be rendered in all its harshness. A sort of truculent meticulousness has been evolved. The universal graciousness of light-flooded nature, the charm of vaguer distances and moving shadows, hardly find place in this regional art which tends to omit everything which belongs to all fair places and more fortunate people and to look rather on the dour and desolate, on uncompromising struggle against or grudging surrender to environment, as really distinctive of the American scene. Thus has been encouraged a manner of frank and vivid ugliness, crass colors and unpatterned shapes, in the expectation that what is coarse must be strong, what is lowly and plebeian must be more truly human, and that thereby will the soul of America find expression.

What shall we say to this latest trend?

Surely, it is on the right track in so far as it is trying to evolve a style of realistic expressionism, creating its mood by recasting the actual American scene into terms that belong specifically and exclusively to painting – not to photography, not to the cinema, not to the eye of the wandering tourist, but only to the painter and the painter's medium; but that its great danger is to fall into the old fallacy, to which all realism is prone, of confusing illustration with art. In illustration, the emotions are those of the scene itself; in pure painting, the emotions are beyond the pictured scene and belong primarily to the art itself, just as the musical emotions belong to the realm of musical experience and only indirectly and by transference to the world of everyday – that realm which the jargon of the army derisively calls "civil life."

The painter's paradox should be plain to every thinking mind: he must picture the world in order to deal with the world's emotions; but the world which he pictures does not merely illustrate those emotions. He does not seek to impart a sense of corporeal frigidity by picturing the snowfields with their blue and purple shadows, nor should he try to instil a sense of the desirability of the American democratic system by picturing an Iowa farm with a well-stocked corn-crib.

Let us pause to survey our situation as we have seen it in historical perspective.

In the past, during some six hundred years from 1300 to 1900 A.D., artists derived their emotional powers from within the Great Tradition of technical evolution. The attainment of realistic illusionism, in so far as the physical medium permits such a thing, ended the Great Tradition and led to the half century of esthetic experimentation. Today the painters who are not still mere researchers or public entertainers for immediate profit and precarious notoriety, being uncertain whither Style is evolving, have sought either to borrow a style which they admired or to create a new style by sheer improvization. But in borrowing a style we cut the flowering branch from the root which nourishes it, and the blossom has withered in our hands; and in improvising a style we discover that we can not arbitrarily and magically produce a medium of emotional significance except in so far as such a medium already exists. There is much to be said for Humpty-Dumpty's trick of using words to suit his own high fancy, and only one apparent inconvenience – nobody else will understand them.

"I don't know what you mean by 'glory,' " Alice said.
Humpty-Dumpty smiled contemptuously. "Of course you don't – till I tell you. I meant 'there's a nice knock-down argument for you'!"
"But 'glory' doesn't mean a 'nice knock-down argument,' " Alice objected.
"When *I* use a word," Humpty-Dumpty said in rather a scornful tone, "it means just what I choose it to mean – neither more nor less."
"The question is," said Alice, "whether you *can* make words mean so many different things."
"The question is," said Humpty-Dumpty, "which is to be master – that's all."

We have been badly put-upon by the Humpty-Dumpties of art, who set shapeless and meaningless things on canvas and then revel in their scorn of us when we admit we do not understand them. There are three terms in the esthetic process – the artist, the work of art, and the audience; and unless all three be operative, there is no art. The sorest point in modern art is its arrogation of importance to the first term at the expense of the other two. This has been the direct result of the cessation of the general tradition within which artists moved. Every artist has had to break his own path. Since Style can not be created overnight or by a single man, the innovators necessarily had recourse to experiment; and since these experiments did not always justify themselves by an effortless success and unlabored intelligibility, their makers had to explain them orally, pamphletize their novelty, philosophize and theorize, carry over into words what had best been left in paint. To this crude esthetic speculation of the artists, the public – notably through the pens of journalists, essayists, and art-critics – have added turgid elucidations of their own. Significantly for the level at which much of this philosophy has been moving, although much of the actual output of these tendentious artists has been straightforward and illuminating esthetic experimentation, neither artist nor spectator has drawn much profit because neither has drawn any of the obvious conclusions. However, by dint of endless repetition, we have gradually undergone a certain amount of healthy esthetic education.

From the extreme practices of realism we have learned that the mere experience of beholding objects, however attractive, does not justify the painter's product. The painter is not holding a mirror to the world, merely to reflect what is already there, but utilizing the world of objects as a focus of recognition and attention, a fabric on which to embroider his designs.

From the impressionists, the cubists, and the futurists we have learned the emotional range of geometrical and other formal resources, have seen in the raw the theoretical harmony and counterpoint of visual art. From non-objective "abstract" art we have learned – or are on the verge of learning – that emotions which are not focussed on the world of ordinary experience are inoperative; they exist, they are perfectly genuine, they may be intense of their kind, but they lack scope and bearing because unrelated to the normal visual world in which our visual emotions reside. They belong to Plato's world of *dianoia*, of supersensuous sense.

From surrealism we have learned that the objective world, which I have just called the necessary focus of recognitional attention, may be freely rearranged and recombined, even to the extent of utter disintegration of its normal physical structure and behavior, but that this can be done only under the very considerable penalty of forsaking the higher levels of conscious experience.

From Negro art and the artistic efforts of children, immature or less mechanically civilized peoples, we have learned that deformations of reality, as we are accustomed to organize it, may be emotionally normal, but must have an inner coherence, a system and sensibility of their own, which usually cuts them off from practical applicability to our own artistic efforts.

But every one of these lessons, though it has enriched our outlook and widened our horizons and above all has taught us tolerance, has been of negative value for the formation of a new Great Tradition. Like the decalogue, these instances tell us mainly what *not* to do. Here is the chapter of their commands:

Do not practice complete realism, else you will be substituting an illustrative document from the outside world for an emotional experience from the world within.

Do not practice complete abstraction, else you will lose every emotional reference to normal human experience; you may attain feeling, but it will be a completely internal feeling, a sort of pleasurable equivalent to cutting your own finger.

Do not follow the surrealists, else you will doom yourself to work with such things as dreams – and lunacies – are made on.

Do not imitate Negroes and children, else you will forfeit your heritage of adolescent maturity.

We have made our tests and trials; we have explored the umbra and penumbra of the luminous Great Tradition of European art; but when it comes to profiting by this most interesting experience, what have we done and what ought we to do?

I have used up my time on the approaches to my theme, judging that to see it in historical perspective was at least to see it in the framework of an abiding truth. In historical perspective the situation of the modern painter is clear. His art is not his own creation, but stretches for centuries behind him. It has been evolved through set phases, dictated by internal necessity, toward a period of emancipation which was reached some fifty years ago. His consequent release from technical tradition has conferred upon the modern painter a freedom which he has not learned to use. The tradition of his craft no longer dictates to him how he shall go; his immediate predecessors have lost themselves in esthetic experiment and so bewildered his public as to leave it powerless to control or guide.

The *optimum desideratum* for contemporary painting is the creation of a style. This can not evolve directly out of its own past behavior, because of the exhaustion of the technical impulse of the Great Tradition and the intervening disruption of a period of free esthetic experiment and unlimited eclecticism. Nor is the extreme present-day appreciation of individualism an incentive to the formation of a new style. Since such a style depends on the united energy of all the artists and all their public, violent individual differentiation is mere eccentricity or exhibitionism. Neither is the present-day public, on whom the artist depends economically for his existence, a good incentive, since the sophisticated portion yields to the typically American fault of demanding to be amused and hence encourages any novelty however absurd, while the great bulk can not rise beyond the illustrative content of art and hence exerts an enormous contrary drag back to realism.

How then shall the new style arise?

First in the process of artistic creation must come the emotional response to the external world. But precisely because the artist seeks to make his feelings articulate so that they may reach and affect other men, the artist's most central problem is the conversion of his emotional apprehension of the world into terms of his art. He cannot paint directly what he feels, primarily because feelings are not made of pigment. It is an equally poor way out merely to paint what he sees, since it is not what he is looking at – which is common property – but the way in which he is able to put this into paint, that distinguishes him from the rest of us. Hence comes his inevitable recourse to that communicatory bond between himself and other human beings, to which I have rather arbitrarily given the name of style.

But style must be a living thing, for within it lurks the continuity which keeps art from dying. And for the artist himself all emotion dissipates unless he can keep his sense – however illusory – of creative power. And hence no style has any strength or hold unless it seems to the artist to be his own attainment, susceptible of growth and change through his own use of it. The style of tomorrow must therefore evolve out of the practice and conventions of today – which means that it will base itself on all the apparent folly of recent and contemporary experimentation, but use this directly as a means of conveying a painter's emotional outlook on his world, becoming its master and not, as today, its slave.

Such a change is sure to come. It is only ordinary destiny that new resources should first be explored through curiosity for what they may contain, then later harnessed to general human needs. Such in the material world has been the history of scientific discovery wherein the useless marvel, often sprung of mere theorizing, becomes adapted to the daily service of mankind. In the less tangible world of the spirit, the laws are not very different; from the capricious vagaries of modern esthetic experiment will be sorted and sifted something to serve our truest needs. What is thus useful, will survive; whatever is merely dishonest and empty, must perish.

This, within my limited vision, limited intellectually, not chronologically, is the only possible basis for creation in the fine arts.

Commentaries

JOSEPH SLOANE

THERE is probably no more difficult subject in the field of art criticism than the one which Dr. Carpenter has so skillfully and ably analyzed. To every lover of art the present status of art is a matter of the gravest concern. The problem is basic; it is also insistent. There are many of us who have been very much troubled by the course which art has taken of late. We dislike, as it were, to find ourselves floating about, anchor gone, amid the choppy waves of cubism, dynamism, futurism, vorticism, suprematism, surrealism, and other "isms" as far as the eye can reach. In this rough water I can also say it has become increasingly difficult for the critic to stand upright, since if he does so, he is in imminent danger of falling overboard into just one of these waves and being drowned.

That the Great Tradition is dead, as explained by Dr. Carpenter, is not, I think, open to serious question. What is more, its passing orphaned a great many able artists who were, willy-nilly, presented with a probably unwanted freedom, and an equally unhappy lack of intelligent support on the part of the public. They went astray, as Dr. Carpenter has pointed out. If you will pardon one more figure of speech, they somewhat resemble a pack of hounds who have lost the scent and have spread out over the countryside sniffing in all directions to see if they may not pick it up. But I differ from Dr. Carpenter who believes that the quarry in this instance is purely style. In other words, does art need to find a style, or does it need to find something which will make style possible?

Dr. Carpenter has spoken at length of the development of technical resource in the representational arts and feels that when this resource had finally been perfected, the Great Tradition, which was really the history of this perfection, came to a close. This is perfectly true, but it is not, I feel, the whole truth about the crisis in art which arose in the middle of the last century, and which still afflicts us now. One interesting subject for discussion would surely be the question as to whether or not the technical process had actually explored all the problems of representation as they are applicable to painting and sculpture. It is true that they seem so to us, but the case may have appeared much the same to the intelligent critic of the eighteen-sixties who was familiar with the meticulous realism of a Meissonier, but was utterly unprepared for the entirely different realism of the Impressionists a few years later.

But the real cause of the end of the Great Tradition seems to lie even deeper than a loss of style or a too great technical knowledge. Dr. Carpenter has shown the necessity for representation in art, but there still remains the further problem of the use to which that representation is put, for in the purpose of representation lies at least one important reason for the creation of art at all.

Limiting ourselves to the more immediate ancestry of modern art, we find that in the Christian West the representational arts have most often been used to express ideas which are made evident through the forms portrayed, but which transcend the more commonly experienced aspects of those forms. The greatest of all these, of course, is the human body. It was through the medium of that form that the great stories of antiquity and the lore of the Church were made apparent to endless generations of men. The thought of the ancient world and the doctrines of the Catholic church were most perfectly adapted to artistic representation and interpretation. Indeed, there were many who never knew of these things through any other medium excepting the spoken word. It was no accident that St. Gregory of Tours favored pictures so that those who could not read might see.

But gradually the human form was no longer capable of symbolizing the dominant thought of the West. The old universality of religious belief broke down before the growing power of Protestantism, a faith which never was a powerful patron of art and was even antagonistic to it. The ideas of the classical world, as they obtained in the Renaissance, were vastly modified, and its mythology became less and less interesting and increasingly removed from the life of the times; and the new ideas of science could find no counterpart in the artist's repertory. The Seventeenth Century witnessed a great and far-reaching change in art; in spite of the genius of a Poussin, the classic spirit dried up into the formalities of the academy. The great Rubens painted the Virgin in the image of his own buxom wife, and Catholic Spain produced one of the greatest artists in her history in the person of Velasquez, who, for all his genius, was no thinker and whose art is almost totally devoid of the imaginative qualities which are essential to a successful painter of ideas. The Great Tradition was already tottering.

Thus the art devoted to the great ideas of antiquity and the Church became devitalized, but at the same time new types were coming into favor, types which were not greatly concerned with ideas, but were content with a simpler subject matter derived from nature and daily life. The roots of such art go far back, but in their pure form they are very scarce before the Sixteenth Century, and not really common until the Seventeenth. Landscape and the various kinds of genre painting were carried to a high state of perfection in France and Holland, and in the latter country displaced both religious and classical subjects almost entirely. Since this type of art was not at the service of any ideology, it could exist in a society whose basic ideas were not really expressible through art forms, in an atmosphere in which the older types began to wither and decay.

The scientific attitude became increasingly common and the art of ideas was hard put to it to hold its position in human esteem. In the middle of the Eighteenth Century religious themes were mentioned as being "boring," and the bones of classical mythology were being picked over for such stray subjects as had hitherto escaped the notice of artists. The period of the French Revolution gave a brief vitality to art devoted to antiquity, but religious art has remained mediocre to this day. The western world put its faith more and more in rational process, scientific inquiry, and the none too satisfactory doctrines of a new and more mechanical economics. To such a world, art had little to offer except beautiful interpretations of the world about or else hollow echoes of a faded tradition dedicated to the nobler ideals and the higher sentiments to which only lip service was paid. Since art could not interpret the ideas of the modern world, it could only turn to the world itself and try to see it with fresh eyes and an open mind. But this attitude was not acceptable to officialdom and the upper bourgeoisie who now found themselves in the rather unfamiliar roles of art patrons. Impregnated with respectability, they clung to the unassailable virtues of an art which, they were told, had presumably been good enough for the greatest previous epochs, and was thus good enough for them.

The result was that the new art movements found themselves in a singularly friendless world. Science and materialism and commerce were poor sources of inspiration. The public would have little to do with an art which actually reflected contemporary life, and as a result many of the more courageous and original spirits turned to these aspects of art which were most purely theirs; namely, the formal qualities and techniques of their craft. In their preoccupation with these matters content and meaning played a decreasingly important part, and in some instances it was omitted altogether.

It would seem, therefore, that art must wait upon a new world of relatively universal ideas which have their basis in the lives of men and not in the colder and more perfect realms of physics, medicine, engineering, and higher mathematics. When and if such a world is made, then art will again move into its older role of confidant and confessor to the world, and with it will come a style fit to express its new ideas.

OSCAR THOMPSON

WITH or without Mr. Harris's consent, affirmation, and blessing, I think that we can say, if only for the sake of engendering something faintly controversial, that we have just heard from a modern composer one of the most eloquent and incisive affirmations of romanticism in music that we are likely to find in our times.

Mr. Harris has given us the central thought that man has created art, as the other works of man have been created, in his own image. Could we have a better fundamental description of what romanticism really means than that thought that man has created art in his own image? What would that mean in music? In music it would mean precisely what Mr. Harris has so painstakingly emphasized and reiterated for us, that man was dealing with his own emotions in the creation of music.

Romanticism, of course, can be defined in many ways. I am not speaking here of a style, of a period, of a species of romanticism that begins with some approximate date in the history of art and suddenly evaporates at some other approximate date. I am speaking of that romanticism which rather defies us to divide art, and particularly music, into such set periods as have troubled many a musical historian. I am speaking of the kind of romanticism that you will find in Mozart as readily as in Beethoven or Weber. I am speaking of the kind of romanticism that you will find in Bach as readily as in Mozart. I am speaking of the kind of romanticism which represents those fundamental emotions that are personal to the individual creator as well as general to humanity.

If I have listened rightly to Mr. Harris, he has found in that realization of personal emotion, that personal emotion which is also a general emotion of all mankind, in that expression of personal emotion, the fundamental basis of artistic creation.

There are three kinds of music if you want to divide music this way. There is the music which is essentially music of emotional appeal. There is another kind of music which is essentially music of a technical or craftsmanship appeal. There is a music which combines in somewhat equal proportions both kinds of appeal. We shall not rightfully dismiss that music which is primarily of technical appeal. Mr. Harris has shown us that the acquirement of a vocabulary is an essential part of a composer's business, and we know that there is music in which the use of the vocabulary for its own sake can be music of a certain appeal, particularly to the technician himself, to his fellow technicians, to all who admire a high degree of skill or perfection in the doing of anything of design and a basic sense of proportion and beauty.

If I have heard Mr. Harris rightly, he has made no appeal here for what in a somewhat abused term is called "pure music." Without knowing his conceptions, we may assume that he is one of those inclined to believe that all so-called pure music is touched with some creative emotion that makes its degree of purity, so-called, something relative.

I have heard, and you have heard, many speak very eloquently for a type of expression in music that fundamentally rests on humanity, on man himself. To anyone who has attempted to deal critically with music of the last forty years, to have a composer of our time deal primarily with that thought, that music is essentially an expression of humanity, is a very heartening thing, because we went through a period when we wondered. We went through a period when there was a certain chorus against that conception of humanity being the really basic thing. We went through a period when new ideas in workmanship, new ideas in the way of saying something, whether that something got back to humanity or not, seemed to dominate our current musical thought. We look back on that period, and as we wonder why so little of music that was most talked about in that period seemed to get beyond relatively small groups of composers who were primarily interested in technical statement, in new ways of doing things, we wonder if we are not putting our finger on the reason for that music not getting beyond the circles of its creators in applying to it what Mr. Harris has told us today.

I remember a meeting of composers who were once the ultra-modern composers, at which one of their number rose to speak, and said that there was a misunderstanding generally accepted about the composers of what was then "today." "Our composers," he said – and remember he was speaking to one of these circles of what might be called technical cultists – "are working in precisely the same spirit and to the same ends as the composers of past periods."

But were they working primarily to express, to represent, to give out what they and their ancestors had absorbed of common humanity? Were they not really writing for each other and for themselves in their preoccupation with certain technical problems, certain conceptions, certain stylistic ideas, and their very special preoccupation of turning over a new leaf and getting away from what had been the previous way of our musical men?

To the best of my knowledge, Mr. Harris was never a composer of one of those groups. I may be mistaken, but I can not recall of any work of his having been put forward at a Congress of the International Composers' Society; I do not recall works of his in our own New York groups. In his music he has exemplified an aloofness from that principle of revolt for revolt's sake, and of turning the page for the sake of turning the page. In hearing his music I have always been conscious of a firm link with the past, although he was writing in this day in the harmonic and other advanced idioms or contradictions to the traditional idiom, such as figured very significantly in one paragraph of his address. This thought that every new step in composition is not in the end something of war with tradition, that it is merely the amplification of tradition, is a thought that will bring comfort to all of those who cannot believe that art must turn somersaults and start all over again or wipe out what has been created and contributed by great masters whose music is loved.

That love must come from an art that represents humanity. The intimate love of the few, the craft-loving craft, is not the love of humanity; that is the love of interested, specialized, advanced musicians. To think that Schumann, to think that Schubert, to think that Wagner, to think that Chopin, to think that Tschaikovsky, to think that any composer who has built a real place in the affections of humankind, must be discarded as old hat because he did not write in a way that pleases the modern technician, is a very disturbing thought to the person who is not himself concerned with technique.

To have a composer of Mr. Harris's eminence and success give to us that basic thought that music is an expression of humanity is for us to be able to retain our love for those composers who did for us express humanity and who had the vocabulary to do it, whether or not that vocabulary conforms with present trends in composition.

This is telling stories out of school, but I remember many years ago Mr. Harris said something to me that he probably has no recollection of saying. There was a little argument about Wagner, and Mr. Harris said to my astonishment then, "I think Wagner set craftsmanship back fifty years, perhaps one hundred years."

I can see now the basis for such a remark. But in closing I want to remember and pass on that Mr. Harris did not say that Wagner, who certainly drew the inspiration of his art from humanity, set back music as an expression of humanity any period of time. He did not say that because Wagner in his time was in revolt against tradition there was anything in that to keep us either from carrying on the tradition of the older composers or accepting whatever it was that Wagner in this revolt added to tradition.